CW01647195

Our story of Saxmundham

An illustrated recollection of history and tales of an East Suffolk Market Town

Richard & Viv Wills Crisp
Kevin & Jane Gale

Contents

INTRODUCTION

The first time I met Richard Wills Crisp, he had invited me to have a coffee at a local cafe.

I had previously volunteered with the Suffolk Local History Council to be the Local Recorder for Saxmundham, noting the goings-on in the parish, taking over this role from Helen Revell.

During that first meeting Richard mentioned that he was disappointed that there had never been a book about the history and tales of Saxmundham. That comment stayed with me for some time and eventually we came to write our 'Story of Saxmundham'. It's fair to say that starting from scratch, it has been a time consuming and challenging project. We decided to make it a pictorial book, and our team have worked together to research and compile our story.

Saxmundham Museum grew from a collection of bygones once displayed in H.G. Crisp's shop on the High Street and, with the help of the volunteers from the local History Society, a Museum charity was formed in 2001. Those volunteers worked hard to develop the building that Tony Flick bought in 2002 on behalf of the Museum and we remain grateful for the continued support we receive from his family.

The Museum opened to visitors in 2004, with an evening that included speeches from Peter Purves, Philip Hope-Cobbold and Richard Wills Crisp.

The membership and committee have changed and evolved over time but the Museum remains an inclusive and friendly place to come for a visit and see the displays on local history.

From our research for this book it has become apparent that some information and dates recorded elsewhere conflict in detail so we have used our best efforts to reconcile our facts. We have tried to be as accurate as we can be but some anomalies may remain.

Our story of a Suffolk market town represents an insight into the history of Saxmundham, the surrounding area and in some cases the experiences of local residents.

Please enjoy our 'Story'.

Kevin Gale
Trustee, Saxmundham Museum

Above right: 1920s

Bottom right: Aerial shot from 1994

Opposite page: The head of a statue of Claudius

THE EARLY YEARS

The first settlement here is thought to have been made by Saxon raiders. There is a delightfully quaint film, created by British Gaumont Educational Films in 1934 and entitled *Town Settlement*, which explains why a town grew up here. It includes some charming animations to depict the Saxon 'invaders' coming up the river from the sea and finding the fertile valley to settle in.

The old English meaning for the town name could simply be Saxon Hill Settlement. Some though explain the name as referring to a Saxon lord by the name of Seizmond but no documentary evidence exists to support that.

Referred to in the Domesday Book of 1086 as Saxmundham, it fell within the Plomesgate Hundred and was included in the land of Roger Bigod.

The records show that before 1066 it was held as a manor by Algar, a thane of King Edward's, with two carucates of land and 40 acres, five villagers, ten smallholders and three slaves. A carucate is the amount of land that a team of eight oxen could plough and work in a year.

Seven free men were added under the patronage of Algar. Another manor of 1,490 acres was held by Northmen, with three acres of meadow, a church and a further 15 acres and other land, the value of which was, in total, 30 shillings.

The most significant Roman find in the area was the bronze head from the statue of Claudius, discovered in the River Fromus in nearby Rendham.

Another Roman artefact was a lamp found in 1967 behind Ashford House on the High Street.

In AD 60 revolt broke out against Roman rule in Britain. Boudicca (Boadicea), queen of the Iceni, and her two daughters were assaulted by Roman soldiers and their property was seized. The Iceni rebelled and destroyed the Roman strongholds of Colchester, London and St Albans. The head was part of the statue of Claudius on horseback which flanked a temple in Colchester.

The Roman Governor considered withdrawing from Britain but regrouped his forces and Boudicca was finally defeated and committed suicide. It was thought that her retreating army may have thrown the head into the river at Rendham in order to rid themselves of evidence. The head was discovered in 1907 by schoolboy Arthur Godbold, who took it home and, after whitewashing it, placed it on the garden wall!

It was sold to a local estate foreman for five shillings (25p). Sixty years later it was sold at Sotheby's for £15,500 and finally ended up in the British Museum in London as one of their prized artefacts.

Recently there was an archaeological dig in the housing development opposite St John's Church on Church Hill. Through trial trenching they found Early Bronze Age pottery, dating back to 1,500 BC. Roman pottery was also found, along with evidence that the River Fromus had once been navigable, hard to believe now!

MARKETS AND FAIRS

Saxmundham has a rich history of markets and fairs.

In 1272 John de Rammesaye was granted a Royal Charter by Henry III for a weekly market and a three day annual fair in August, at the time of the Feast Day of St John the Baptist.

So successful was the Saxmundham Market in 1275, that complaints were made due to the 'consequential harm to the said town of Orford which is the lord King's, and of the damage to the King himself'.

A further market charter was granted in 1310 by Edward II to Thomas de Verlay, Lord of the Manor. This was 'For good service which he has bestowed and continues to bestow on us.'

Thomas de Verlay received the profit of the market and fair, held on seven acres of land in the town. Toys, pedlery etc. were sold on Whit Tuesday and a hiring for servants was held on the Thursday before Old Michaelmas Day.

The location of the seven acres may have been the current Market Place, stretching past the site of the Railway Station in Albion Street towards the Mill.

In 1336 Saxmundham was known as 'Saxmundham Market', similar to how nearby Wickham Market is known today.

In 1346 Sir John de Wingfield, one of the English Knights who fought alongside Edward III at the battle of Crecy, was awarded a charter to hold a Fair on 24th June, the day that the Nativity of St John was celebrated. Sir John de Wingfield was also at the capture of Calais in 1347.

The weekly market day was moved to Wednesday as the traditional Thursday was clashed with the Woodbridge market and damaged trade.

There were stocks in the market, and a pillory which was owned by Hannah Dowsing. This was demolished in 1830.

Opposite page and far left: The original position of the Pump in the Market Place

Left: The pump's location along Rendham Road in 2000, with the water tower in the background, before it was relocated in Market Place

Right: Market Place in the 1950s

Right: Market Day in the 1960s and 1970s

People congregate outside the Bell Hotel on market day

Flicks' annual lamb sale was held in Ben Coopers' meadow in Kelsale Road (North Entrance), the animals coming in on foot. In its first year, 1867, there were 4,000 entries, falling to 600 for the final sale in 1942.

Right: The fair comes to Saxmundham, 1920s

A new town pump, made at Garrett's of Leiston, was presented by Squire William Long in 1838 and located in Market Place.

By the year 2000, the pump had been moved close to the Water Tower on Rendham Road and was later moved again to its present position near the Market Place car park.

Flick & Sons' livestock market, behind the White Hart, made Saxmundham a central and important centre for trading livestock, tools and other hardware.

Livestock would be driven through the town to the market and the roadside drains would be boarded up to make sure the animals didn't get stuck.

The local railway had a branch line down to Snape where a trader could send stock to Snape quay to be loaded onto barges and exported. Local farm produce included sugar beet. The livestock market closed in January 1987 and relocated to Campsea Ashe. The old site was redeveloped and is now home to the store of a national supermarket chain.

Above left: Bids being made in the cattle ring

Above right: Cattle pens

In the background, the White Hart public house.

It's interesting to note the green fence between the pub grounds and the market site. This boundary would eventually be disputed between the local land owners.

Left: Inside the auction room

PUBS AND INNS

THE ANGEL Market Place

A 16th century timber framed building in Market Place housed the Angel inn.

Local figures such as Richard Stopher often held public auctions in the Angel as it was one of the largest buildings in Saxmundham.

In the 19th Century, the Angel was a staging point for stagecoaches travelling between London and Halesworth and for coaches meeting the London steamers calling at Ipswich.

One of the daily tasks at the inn was to sweep up the sand from the floor, sieve out the debris and put the sand back down.

In 1928, Tom Compton had a shop in the yard selling shellfish and caged canaries.

After The Angel closed for business in 1976, the building was bought by Suffolk Coastal District Council and was converted to several dwellings and small business premises.

Right: James Woolnough

Below: The Angel entrance in Market Place and the back yard

Landlords included:

1780 - John Woodcock, who left in his will an annuity of £150 to his wife and £3000 to each of his 12 children.

1861 - James Woolnough

1954 - Mona Emsden. Mona told the tale of a large dinner at the Angel in the 1940s, where the host disappeared without paying the bill!

WHITE HART High Street

Earliest records identify Samuel Sustenance as landlord in 1784.

Over the years it operated as a Commercial & Posting House, while John Lincoln was landlord, a car hire and taxi service run by James Forsdike, and a meeting place for the local Cycle Club in the late 1930s.

Leslie Owen Clarke succeeded his uncle James Forsdike as landlord in 1925.

The White Hart ran as a pub and restaurant until the late 1990s.

Was the landlord's father a spy?

Samual Forsdike, father of James, landlord of the White Hart from 1912, was locked up in Russia for four years as a suspected spy.

The family were also tallow merchants, with their company Orwell Soap & Candle Works based in Ipswich and Rostoff.

Below: Samual Forsdike

Below left: James Forsdike stands in the doorway in 1914, with taxis lined up in front

Above: Leslie Clarke in 1919

Left: The Cycle Club

QUEEN'S HEAD High Street

The Queens Head is mentioned in the Ipswich Journal of 1757 where the "The Three Tuns or Queens Head" is offered for let. Also mentioned is an acre of land behind the pub. The landlord in 1796 was a J. Simpson, when the Queen's Head was classified as a Public House. From 1855 to 1885 it was classified as a Posting House, becoming a Hotel in 1888 when the landlord, Walter Balls, advertised the hotel as having 'Wines and Spirits of the finest quality, well-aired beds, lock-up stables and coach house, excellent bowling green and quoit ground.'

Harry Cable, in 1895, drove the horse omnibus to collect guests from the railway station.

In 1892 the Oddfellows Guild met regularly in the Queen's Head until 1922 when they built their own premises in Fairfield Road, now a private House.

Smith & Wesby's garage was located in the yard behind. In 1915 they moved to a smart new building in South Entrance.

A large upstairs function room was regularly hired for dinner dances, large meetings and discos. Landlord Percy Hubbard's son Geoff, leader of the Melody Makers Dance Band, played here in 1937. A well-known character in the town, Geoff went on to establish Hubbard's Electricals, a local chain of shops.

Popular landlords from 1955 to 1967, Ted and Milly Ballard, put on a fine Harvest Festival display and supper in the upstairs room, and this became a regular feature in the town.

Milly Ballard later became the first warden/ manager of the newly built old people's flats at Swan House in Saxon Road.

In 2003 the Queen's Head became a Thai Restaurant and take-away but with the southern bar remaining.

Top right: High Street, Queen's Head sign can be seen on the left

Centre right: Ted and Milly Ballard's Harvest Festival display

Bottom right: Smith & Wesby's garage at the back of the Queens Head, before moving to South Entrance (far right)

Background: High Street

MARKET HALL and BELL INN High Street

The current Bell Hotel replaced an earlier inn which had burnt down. Early records show a Blue Bell Inn in Saxmundham, (1712-1714), with landlord Robert Mean.

King George II visited the Bell Inn on January 7th in 1737 on his way to London from Lowestoft.

"During the years 1842-3, a company of shareholders, at the cost of £11,000, rebuilt the Bell Inn, renamed "hotel", which had been destroyed by fire, and also erected a commodious Corn Exchange, and a large Public Room adjoining.

The two latter divided by a moveable partition, and could be opened out into one apartment, 106' long, and 32' in height and breadth."

From Whites 1844, Suffolk

Unfortunately, during the re-building programme, the shareholders ran out of money for the Corn Exchange, which later became known as The Market Hall. They appealed to Squire Long of Hurts Hall to help them out. He agreed, and the grateful townsfolk of Saxmundham presented him with a silver ink stand which can be seen at the Museum along with a list of all the subscribers and their donations.

Above: Market Hall with original railings

The Bell Hotel, together with the Corn Exchange, was sold in 1845. The Corn Exchange did not officially open until 1846, with one of its features being the new lantern roof.

Above: The badge of the Suffolk Cyclists Club can be seen above the Bell's front door; the club committee dined there and the cyclists attended the local Clarke's Tearooms

To Innkeepers Merchants, and builders.

PARTICULARS

OF THAT

VALUABLE AND EXTENSIVE PROPERTY

KNOWN AS

THE BELL INN,

WITH

PUBLIC ROOM,

AND ABOUT

Six Acres of fine Pasture Land,

SITUATE IN THE CENTRE OF THE MARKET TOWN OF

SAXMUNDHAM,

Commanding delightful Prospects for Building

TO BE SOLD BY AUCTION,

BY

GIRLING AND SON,

UPON THE PREMISES,

On FRIDAY, the 14th day of November, 1845,

AT ONE O'CLOCK IN THE AFTERNOON.

IN EIGHTEEN LOTS.

The Property may be viewed, and Particulars and Conditions of sale, withLithographic Plans, had on application to Mr. Benjamin Moulton, Land Surveyor, Woodbridge ; Messrs. Mayhew and Son, Solicitors, Saxmundham ; the Auctioneers, Peasesnhall, near Yoxford ; and at the Inns, in the Neighbourhood.

BRGHTLEY, PRINTER, SAXMUNDHAM.

Left: Sale brochure (front page) for the Bell Inn, 1845

Land behind the Bell was offered as several individual plots with suggestions for building and development

As a coaching inn for the Mail Coach and in the 1840s being the only posting office in Saxmundham, it was an important stage on the London to Great Yarmouth route. It received four visiting coaches each day, two up and two down. The Bell had 40 stables and was required to always have fresh horses ready for the coaches.

A passenger service from London, by the Original Blue company, ran between London and Yarmouth.

Once the railway came to Saxmundham the coaching service became unprofitable and was discontinued. An Old Blue coach was left at the Bell, stored under a lean-to shed which, in the 1950s, eventually collapsed, destroying the old coach.

The six-acre Bell meadow hosted the annual Lambsale, before the sales moved to the other end of the town, as well as agricultural shows which later moved to Hurts Hall.

In the 1960s a guest staying at the Bell complained one morning about the old lady who had come into his room, tucked him in and poured water into a washing bowl. The man was shocked when the staff told him that no such person existed but it may have been the ghost thought to haunt the Bell Hotel since the fire that destroyed the old Inn!

Over the decades the Market Hall has been extensively used, including the annual Museum Quiz Night!

1879

An inquest was held at the Market Hall after Clara Barber was found in state of high distress, declaring that her child had fallen into the well at her dwelling, formally known as the "Bottle and Glass" pub. She was presented to the coroner as a potential murderer but a witness confirmed that he had seen the child play and climb around the well. The case was dismissed but the mother was ruled to have become insane with grief.

1899

A Bachelor's Dance was held. Gentlemen would book a dance and write their names in the programme.

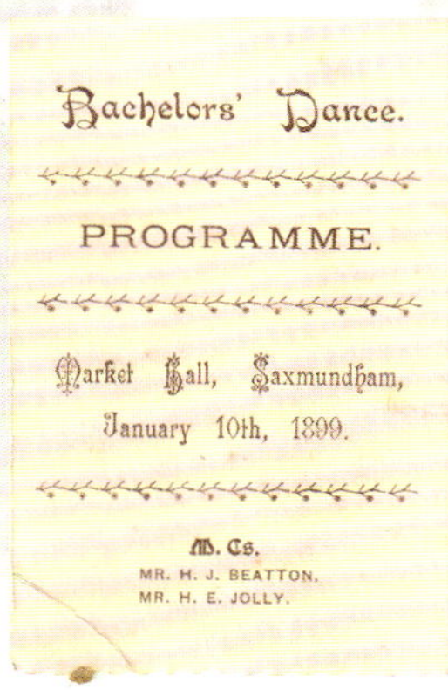

Bachelors' Dance.

PROGRAMME.

Market Hall, Saxmundham,
January 10th, 1899.

M. Cs.
MR. H. J. BEATTON.
MR. H. E. JOLLY.

1905

Dame Clara Butt, with her husband Kennerley Rumford, gave a concert. They sang The Keys of Heaven to the delight of the townsfolk of Saxmundham. It was recorded that the carriages of the gentry lined the High Street.

1910

When the Suffolk Show was held on The Layers in Saxmundham, the Market Hall hosted the sale of teas and Fancy Goods.

1913

Eliza Comes to Stay was performed by the Marchioness of Graham of Euston Park, with her friends and family.

1913

The Suffragists (the first wave of campaigners for rights and votes for women) marched from Yarmouth to Hyde Park. On July 15th they arrived in Saxmundham and held a rally in the Market Place.

Above: Entertainers Dame Clara Butt and Kennerley Rumford

Far right: Saxmundham's ladies selling refreshments; High Street decorations for the Suffolk Show. Interesting to note, the six pointed star was often used for decoration

Right: Bachelors' Dance Programme

This was followed by a tea in the Market Hall. The Suffragists then set off on 16th July arriving at Hyde Park on 26th July where a crowd of over 50,000 was addressed by Mrs Millicent Fawcett (sister of Dr Elizabeth Garrett Anderson of Aldeburgh).

1914

Officers and men were entertained on Christmas Day.

1937

Kelly's Directory states "The Market and Corn Hall will seat 250 persons. The market for grain is held here on Wednesdays. The County Court is held here every alternate month with Magistrates Meetings every other Thursday".

1954

Having held dance classes for all ages for three decades, Kay Goddard and husband Dennis Page put on a production of *Show Business* at the Market Hall.

Top: Oddfellows Centenary Lunch, 1910

Centre: Christmas 1914 dinner for the army officers; note the 'Lantern' roof

Bottom: Kay Goddard and pianist Merle Adams being presented with bouquets

A local lad recalls hanging round the Bell during the 1950s and getting paid a few pennies to help set-up and take back the market stalls which were stored in the sheds at the back of the Bell. The stall holders would congregate in the 'Bell Tap', an out-building bar area, as the workers were discouraged from entering the main building.

The main saloon bar used to be the long room to the right of the building and there are reminiscences of this being used to host 'gentlemen's evenings.'

1957

Wilfred Pickles hosted his national radio show *Have a Go* from the Market Hall, with a ballot for tickets. The pianist on the show later found fame as 'Betty' in the ITV's *Coronation Street.*

In the 1980s a development company tried to formulate plans to demolish the Market Hall and the Gannon Rooms and replace them with a concrete built shopping centre.

2013

On July 15th a commemorative event with speeches and tea was held for the centenary of the Market Hall.

Right: Remembrance Day service outside the Market Hall

"Have a go"

Twenty million people, according to Wilfred Pickles, would hear the broadcast from Saxmundham Market Hall and the recorded programme the following Sunday, 15th December 1957.

This popular radio show of the fifties caused much interest and response from local people when 'Wilfred and Mable came to town'. And the evening proved to be a highly successful event.

Before the singing of 'God Save Our Queen', which ended every public performance in those days, Mrs A Aldous thanked Mr. Pickles for bringing to Saxmundham "a united happiness which is spread over wide circles".

The chosen six contestants on the evening were as follows:

Mrs Mable Flatman - housewife
Mr Alfred Woolnough - agricultural worker
Miss Elizabeth Shelley - worker at the glass factory
Mr Maurice Bugg - motor mechanic (with Mr Harry Lyon in a duet)
Miss Janet Howard - shop assistant
Mr Alfred Akers - grocer

The jackpot went to Mr Akers. It consisted of fifty shillings, a Suffolk ham, Suffolk rusks, a pound of Saxmundham sausages and a jar of Suffolk Blackballs.

The British Broadcasting Corporation & Mr Wilfred Pickles request the pleasure of your company at the Local Broadcast of "Have a Go"

183 (For details see counterfoil)

P.T.O.

"Have a Go" was hosted by Wilfred and Mabel Pickles and Harry Hudson. Another regular host and pianist was Violet Carson, later the household name of Ena Sharples of Coronation Street. The show lives on in our memories helped by such phrases as "Have a go!" and "Put it on the table, Mabel!".

"Give her the money, Mabel!" Mabel hands over 'the money' to Mrs M Flatman whilst Wilfred Pickles cracks a joke.

LAW AND ORDER

The ceremonial staff of office, or tipstaff, was used by a Saxmundham Town official, probably the High Constable or Beadle. It was first used during the reign of James II in 1687.

The crown at the top could be unscrewed to reveal the 'staff' - a warrant appointing the holder of the Tipstaff to their position of authority.

Policing in Suffolk changed little between the 12th and early 19th centuries. It remained dependent on the age old system of a Justice of the Peace, Constable and Town Watchman.

The Constabulary Force for the Eastern Division of Suffolk was established in 1840. The headquarters were at Saxmundham Police Station with Saxmundham man, John Hatton, in charge.

The Force comprised the Chief Constable, Deputy Chief Constable, two superintendents, four inspectors and 72 constables, all stationed in 72 districts.

1853 : Constable James King in charge in Saxmundham.

1855 : John Hatton (Chief Constable for the division) lived at Carlton House.

1863 : Police station in Albion Street built, residence for one police officer, one cell and one room for magistrates.

1868 : Arthur Page in charge.

The town beadle in 1895 was Robert Wooltorton who was also the jeweller at 23 High Street. The jewellers served as an early police station and the cells remained in the basement. The original beadle stick can be seen in the museum along with an original cell door.

Also in the museum is the sword-stick presented in 1911 to PC Charles Revell of Sweffling.

Local Crime and Punishment

Samuel Morsley of Albion Street was charged in February 1846 with fraudulently obtaining a land drain spade to the value of seven shillings from W. Wells ironmongers. At his trial at Woodbridge Sessions, the chairman pointed out that he had previously been convicted of stealing a scythe. Perhaps surprisingly he was let off with a warning and released from custody.

Unfortunately Samuel did not heed the warning! In July 1846 he was arrested and charged with stealing a scythe and scythe stick from William Woods of Saxmundham. This time he was sent to the Suffolk Summer Assizes where he was sentenced to be transported to Australia for seven years.

Above: The Beadle's Tipstaff

Left: The original cell in the basement at 23 High Street (currently a jewellers); the cell door can been seen in the Museum

Background: Saxmundham Police, 1900s

Smuggling

In the 1740s the landlord of the Bell Inn, J. Southwell, was also the local excise officer.

In order to enforce the law, and to ensure excise duty would be collected on imported goods, contingents of dragoons were billeted around the local towns and villages but the inns involved in the smuggling would make sure their in-house soldiers would be drunk when the smugglers transported their contraband.

One evening a witness saw over 60 horses loaded with tea, brandy and gin coming away from Sizewell Gap.

On another occasion a revenue officer based at Saxmundham heard about smuggling. He guessed that the smugglers would move the contraband to Leiston or to Aldringham, probably to the Parrot and Punchbowl. He was right. He rode to the pub with two (sober) dragoons, and caught the smugglers red-handed.

There are tales of hidden tunnels underneath the town and a confirmed local tunnel is one that leads away from the parish church at nearby Sweffling down towards the building that had once been the village inn.

Toll Gate

In 1663 the first Turnpike Act was introduced. This entailed erecting gates across the country where tolls could be collected, financing the improvement of roads. Gatekeepers notoriously defrauded their employers whilst at the same time 'fleecing' the traveling public.

In Saxmundham, Isaac Ablett, carpenter, and John Booth, bricklayer, were engaged to build a toll gate and a toll house near the north end of Saxmundham for £93. The toll gate opened in 1792.

Right: Tollgate cottage, early 1900s

Ipswich to Yarmouth turnpike tolls:

"For every horse, mule, ass, or other beast drawing any type of coach, chariot, landau, barouche, sociable, vis-a-vis, phaeton, Berlin chaise, chaise marine, curricle, calash, cabriolet, van, caravan, chair, gig, whiskey or hearse or any such like carriage, the sum of 3d".

Needless to say, travellers tried to find alternative routes to avoid the turnpike Toll gates!

The building of the turnpike also allowed Samuel Long, owner of Hurts Hall and as chairman of the local Turnpike committee, the opportunity to divert the route of the southern entrance into Saxmundham away from the Hall. He demolished several buildings to increase his parkland, including the former residence of Reverend Bigsby, hence the name of the southern road junction still known as Bigsby's Corner.

ARTISTS AND ARTISANS

Henry Bright 1810-1873

Henry Bright was the son of Saxmundham clockmaker Jerome Bright (1770-1846) and Susannah Denny of Alburgh, Norfolk. The family lived above their business premises at Ashford House in the High Street, .

The youngest of nine children, Bright attended Owen Haxell's 'School for Young Gentlemen' in North Entrance (now Brook Cottage). It is believed that Thomas Thurlow was a fellow pupil.

The family were strict non-conformists and regularly attended chapel in Rendham.

At the age of twelve he left school and moved to Woodbridge as a chemist's apprentice. His artistic hopes were to be fulfilled when, having been transferred to a Norwich chemist, his indentures were passed to artist Alfred Stannard of Norwich. He received lessons from John B. Crome and John Sell Cotman, both leading members of the Norwich Society of Artists.

In 1833 Henry Bright married Eliza Brightly and they moved to London in 1836.

Predominantly landscape, his works were exhibited widely and at the Royal Academy. He embarked on annual 'sketching trips', touring the UK and parts of Europe.

Queen Victoria bought one of his paintings and he was a close friend of J.M.W. Turner. He became a teacher to the upper classes and the aristocracy. Among his pupils were the Grand Duchess Marie of Russia, and the daughter of Sir Robert Peel. His annual income exceeded £2,000, equivalent to approximately £160,000 today.

Due to ill health he returned to Saxmundham in 1858 and lived in Park Cottage but his last few years were spent with his niece in Ipswich where he continued to paint until his death.

'For splendid sky effects Bright was second only to Turner. In some pictures the sky is surcharged with heavy clouds, and the portrayal of rain is singularly powerful ...

Obituary, Suffolk Chronicle 27-9-1873

Above: Henry Bright

Left: North Beach, Great Yarmouth

Thomas Thurlow 1813-1899

Thomas was the fifth of six children born to master builder John Thurlow (1785-1850) and Rebecca of Framlingham. John built several houses in Saxmundham, including their family home 'The White House' just off the High Street (now 'Holly Lodge').

Thomas Thurlow attended four schools, including a preparatory school in Saxmundham run by 'Bogy' Smith and a 'School for Young Gentlemen' in North Entrance run by Owen Haxell, known as 'Custards'. At the age of 13 he began assisting his father in the masonry and building business.

His artistic career began with the designing and making of many articles in plaster and wood, even to the extent of a violin which was described in later years as being 'of fine tune'. He was commissioned to create many designs, as well as countless sculptures in a range of media. Although he considered himself an amateur painter, his portraits were highly acclaimed, not least his collection of 'Aldbro Worthies', fishermen and other local characters.

With little formal training in sculpture, he moved to London in 1836, where he worked at a masonry shop in Regent Street and at the London Marble Works.

In 1838 he returned to Suffolk to open a business, first in Halesworth and then in 1839 in Saxmundham, receiving commissions from The Hon. Sophia North at Great Glemham Hall and William H. Long of Hurts Hall.

Not everyone, however, appreciated his work. He exhibited 'The Reclining Cupid' in an Ipswich art exhibition and received criticism from the local press: "Thurlow's cupid ... Looks very stupid"! A few years later the aforesaid cupid was sold at Christies for 34 guineas.

His work was exhibited in Ipswich and Norwich and at the Royal Academy from 1844. In that same year he married, and entered fully into public matters in the town.

His detailed drawing of an engine for Garrett's of Leiston was eventually used to make up the first ever portable engine at the engineering works.

Works that can be seen locally include a bust of poet Crabbe, at St Peter & St Paul's Church, Aldeburgh, the reredos for St John's, Saxmundham, and Aldeburgh Church, a life-size statue in Caen stone at St Mary & St Peter's Church, Kelsale, a memorial at Yoxford Church, a monument in the church at Benacre, a Gothic monument at Theberton Church, a marble bust of Richard Garrett at Leiston Church and stone pulpits at Debach Church and others.

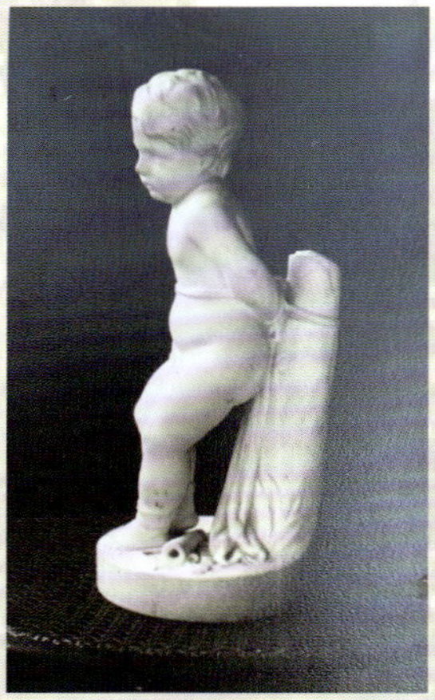

Top: Bust of Richard Garrett at Leiston

Above and right: 'Cupid Bound' and bust of Suffolk poet Crabbe

William Talbot 1823-1907

Examples of William Talbot's paintings can be seen in Saxmundham Museum. Talbot lived in Ada Cottage, Albion Street.

John Gray 1869-1951

Landscape artist John Gray lived in Benhall with his wife Dulcibella. He was a member of the Royal Academy, the Royal Society of British Artists, Ipswich Art Club and the Royal Society of Painters in Water Colour.

He was also a well-known snowdrop enthusiast with a flower later named in his honour.

He died at Benhall Cottage in 1951, aged 82.

A leaflet is available in the museum.

Above: William Talbot, Self-portrait, Haywain in a Country Lane, Suffolk River Scene

Left: John Gray

HURTS HALL

The Manor of Hurts has existed for centuries alongside the Manors of Swans and Wingfield.

The builders of the last two incarnations of the Hall were the Long family who owned plantations in the Caribbean.

Samuel Long greatly extended the surrounding parkland and was responsible for extending the Hurts Hall park lands by demolishing several buildings, including a pub called the Coach and Horses. One house, known at the time as the Old Parsonage, was last occupied by the Reverend Bigsby before it too was pulled down. Hence the name for Bigsby's Corner at the road junction of Sternfield, Benhall and Saxmundham.

The lake was filled in following the death of a child after being bitten by a mosquito.

Above: Drawing created and published by H. Davy of Ipswich in July 1857

Right: William Beeston Long, aged 15

Further land was reclaimed as the Town Marshes were drained and a water course dug for the river Fromus. The Hall had its own running water system with water drawn from a well by a pump powered by a small windmill.

The 1890 fire

During one Saturday night a fire broke out and the mansion was reduced to ashes. For nearly a month Col. Long had been absent from the house.

The fire was noticed at about midnight by William Newson, walking home to Farnham, and the Saxmundham Fire Brigade was called. By 1.20 am the Fire Brigade was at work using the park reservoir and 700ft of hose, first attacking the flames at the front, and then at the rear. A number of locals arrived to lend a helping hand. The main effort was saving the furniture of which the greater part was carried out safely onto the lawn, overseen by Mr. J. Ashford.

'The fire burned away fiercely and furiously.'

Just after 3am the roof fell in and by 6am the destruction of the front block of the mansion was complete.

The cause of the fire could not be ascertained, but some plumbers had been cleaning the paint off the front windows, using large 'flamers' and 'probably fired some of the internal woodwork unobserved'.

20th Century

The estate was requisitioned by the army during WWII and the Hall was a venue for several high-level meetings, including a D-Day planning meeting with Winston Churchill, Eisenhower and Montgomery.

Since then Hurts Hall has been owned by Mrs. Aline Aldous, Hubert Meadows, Col. Ron and Mrs. Mavis Warren and currently by Roger and Wendy Skinner.

Ice carnival

During the severe winter of 1890/91 an ice carnival was held.

'The 56th day since the commencement of the severe cold, January 19th, was suitably marked by a skating Fête. A procession of about 90 torch bearers, most of whom were dressed in strange costumes, headed by the band, marched the whole length of the town, and then turning back entered Hurts Hall Park by the lodge, and passed on to the river at the bridge. There the procession, preceded by some horsemen and a sledge, made its way along the ice, in the middle of which a large bonfire was burning. The flickering light of the fire, the torches planted along the sides of the river, upon which many skaters were moving rapidly about, and some coloured lights formed a most picturesque scene, and will not readily be forgotten by the great crowds who witnessed it.'

Saxmundham Parish Magazine, Feb 1891

The park hosted various public activities including the Suffolk Show on 14 occasions and holding the second oldest lawn tennis tournament on 'the cricket pitch'. There is also mention of the town football club having free use of a pitch.

Above: The interior of the Hall in 1958

Below: The restored Hall in 2021

SUFFOLK SHOW

For a number of years local agricultural shows had been held on the six acre meadow of The Blue Bell Inn.

In 1831 the East Suffolk Agricultural Association was formed following a meeting at Wickham Market and, under the presidency of the Earl of Stradbrooke, the first Association show was held the following year, also at Wickham Market.

For the next 13 years the East Suffolk shows were held alternately at Wickham Market and Saxmundham, before moving to venues around the county.

In 1856 East Suffolk merged with West Suffolk to form the Suffolk Agricultural Association.

The Suffolk Show was often held on the estate of the current association President. Hurts Hall's Aline Aldous recalls in one of the Museum's oral histories that it was a wonderful opportunity to visit the other estates.

On the occasions when the show was held on Saxmundham Layers, the town was magnificently decorated, as shown here.

The practice of moving the Suffolk Show around the county continued until, in 1959, a 130 acre site was purchased on Bucklesham Road, Ipswich to form a permanent Suffolk show ground, later renamed as Trinity Park.

Right, from top:

A bi-plane suspended in front of the bank in Market Place, 1910

President Capt Cobbold presents prizes to P Adams for Best Suffolk Mare and to Sir Guy Hambling's stock-man for Best Red Poll Bull, 1939

Machinery Stand, 1939

Saxmundham Town Band, 1925

LES COSAQUES DJIGUITES

Archaeological surveys of The Layers, the area south of the town, revealed 'enclosures' and it's thought that The Layers are so called because herdsmen driving livestock to Saxmundham market would 'lay-up' their stock there before market day.

Following the Russian revolution, having fought against the communists, The Cossacks had to leave and settled in other parts of Europe. They put on displays of their fine horsemanship that proved very popular. They eventually split into three groups - one went to North America and featured in several films, one stayed in mainland Europe while the third came to England. Les Cosaques Djiguites in England were commanded by Captain Korolkoff, touring many locations including Saxmundham's Layers and featuring in the Suffolk Show in 1939.

Right: Programme for The Cossacks' performance in Saxmundham

Below and background: Cossacks performing on The Layers

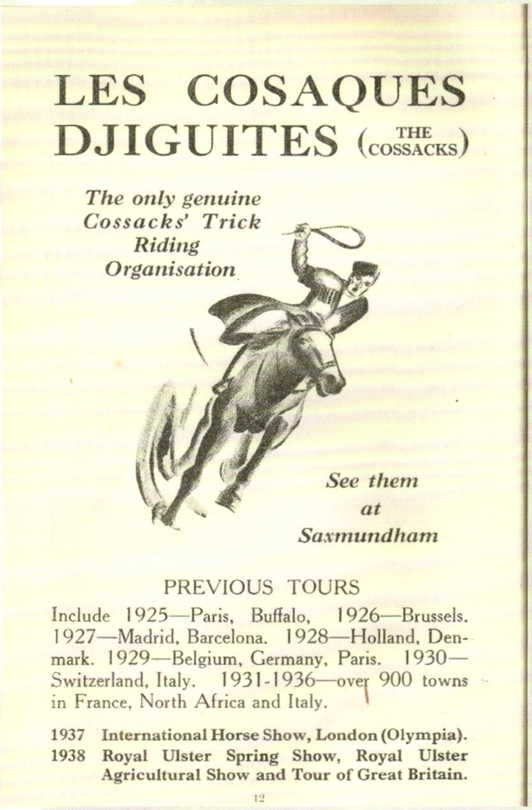

LES COSAQUES DJIGUITES (THE COSSACKS)

The only genuine Cossacks' Trick Riding Organisation

See them at Saxmundham

PREVIOUS TOURS

Include 1925—Paris, Buffalo, 1926—Brussels. 1927—Madrid, Barcelona. 1928—Holland, Denmark. 1929—Belgium, Germany, Paris. 1930—Switzerland, Italy. 1931-1936—over 900 towns in France, North Africa and Italy.

1937 International Horse Show, London (Olympia).
1938 Royal Ulster Spring Show, Royal Ulster Agricultural Show and Tour of Great Britain.

12

After WWII many Cossacks were forcibly repatriated to Soviet forces who executed them as traitors. The fear of the post-war British Government was that liberated men would not be returned if the Cossacks were not sent back.

It had been thought for many years that the former England-based Cosaques Djiguites had suffered this mortal fate but later it was found that Captain Korolkoff and some of his troop had settled in Bedfordshire and now rest, buried in a church yard at Aspley Guise near Milton Keynes.

RAILWAY STATION

The footbridge (below) was often frequented by eager train-spotters. They were particularly excited when a Britannia Class train came through!

The Station at Saxmundham opened on 1st June 1859.

The 'Up' platform was adjacent to the Station and with the goods yard opposite, the 'Down' platform was 'offset' to the south, across the road. The moveable platform was built into the south crossing gate in 1874 to accommodate longer mainline trains but was destroyed in 1963 when a freight train crashed through it.

Originally there was a goods shed and yard. Cargo could be sent South to London or North to the Northern coast.

A branch line to Snape meant cargo could be transported to the barges moored at the quayside.

On 23rd February 1956 the Aldeburgh branch line snowed up. A snow plough was brought from Lowestoft to clear the line in time for the 12.50 arriving from Aldeburgh!

The station house has hosted many businesses, including a restaurant, but was badly damaged by fire in 2008 and is currently in the process of being restored.

Main picture and Far left: Saxmundham Railway Station

Near left: Snow plough, 1956

Above from top: Covered footbridge; Raymond Green receives token from driver; single track Aldeburgh branch line

LOCAL PEOPLE

Margery Beddingfield 1742-1763

Margery Beddingfield, murderer of her husband John, a farmer in Sternfield, was one of the last women in England to be sentenced to be burnt for 'petty treason'. Her offence was plotting the murder of her husband.

Right: Justice being carried out

Background: Sternfield Church

The dead husband was buried in Sternfield churchyard, judged to have suffered an accidental death by falling out of bed.

The actual murder was committed by farm-hand Richard Ringe who was urged to the crime by Margery, who promised him marriage. The two later fell out and each made confessions about their parts in the affair.

Both prisoners were tried for murder and petty treason, the justification for the latter charge being that the deceased was the master of one and husband of the other.

Both Richard and Margery were found guilty and sentenced to death, she by burning and he by hanging, his body to be dissected. The sentences were carried out at Rushmere St Andrew, two miles out of Ipswich, where the gallows stood on the right hand side of the Woodbridge road just over the borough boundary.

On 8th April 1763, the condemned pair were drawn on a sledge to the place, where Richard was hanged, but Margery was strangled before being burnt.

John Shipp 1784-1834

John Shipp was born on 16th March 1784 in North Entrance, Saxmundham. His mother died while John was still young and while his father was away as a soldier of fortune, possibly in America.

John and his brother were left to fend for themselves and relied upon the Parish to support them. At the age of nine, John saw his brother join a man-of-war and never heard from him again.

John was so fascinated by soldiers, he lied about his age and signed up for an experimental boy-soldier regiment. Shipp's daring exploits and feats of bravery while serving in India are so numerous that many have gone unrecorded officially and are only known because they were repeated by returning soldiers.

He was eventually pensioned out of the army after thirty years, finally leaving India.

His reputation arrived in England well before him, ensuring him 'cult' status. He was much sought after as a speaker and adored by women. His memories live on in the many books and plays that he published in the early Victorian era.

Flogging and its Substitute: a Voice from the Ranks, was in the form of a letter to Sir Francis Burdett, being a powerful indictment of the detestable barbarities of the cat o' nine tails, which, as the author maintained, 'flogged one devil out and fifty devils in.' Burdett sent the writer the sum of £50, and most of his suggestions were adopted by the military authorities.

As recently as 1980 his books were still being reprinted. The popular television series of the 1990s, *Sharpe*, was inspired, in part, by the life and adventures of this extraordinary man.

Left: John Shipp

Thomas Cooper

In 1802, a young Thomas Cooper was "before the mast" on the brig *Adventure* when he was suddenly promoted to Ship's Mate by Captain William Codling and then ordered to drill holes into the hull of the ship with the aim of sinking her.

The crew were rescued and Cooper, fearing for his own life, fled first to London and then walked to Saxmundham where he was met by his mother and sister before handing himself in and giving evidence against his captain.

Codling was found to have taken out a £700 insurance policy on the brig. William Codling stood trial for defrauding the insurance underwriters, and, as a capital offence, when found guilty was hanged at Portsmouth.

The Stilts-Man

Alfie Proudfoot, also known locally as the Stilts-man, would climb out of a first floor window in Market Place where he had his groceries and sweets shop, and step onto his stilts, placed against the building in readiness. He was a popular attraction at local celebrations.

Right: Saxmundham's stilts-man, Alfie Proudfoot

Benjamin Rowe

The town's coal merchant lived in the house by the entrance to Harpers Lane. Mr. Rowe's coal depot was situated on the site which is now the town car park.

Wallace Brundish and the Zeppelin

Herbert Brundish was employed as a carpenter by Gibbs & Rodwell, whose premises were at the rear of what was Mitchells Garage in the High Street. Herbert signed indentures to Gibbs & Rodwell in 1898, binding him to five years' service at two shillings a week for year one, increased at the rate of one shilling per year until the end of his apprenticeship.

Wallace Herbert Brundish, son of Herbert and Clara Brundish, was for a time a gardener at Hurts Hall. He recalls from his childhood, during WW1, being grabbed out of bed as a huge Zeppelin hovered over the outskirts of Saxmundham but then burst into flames and drifted away over Carlton Park to crash at Theberton. He was taken to see the crash site the next day.

He remembers too the town policeman, Sgt. Chapman, cycling around the town, blowing his whistle and calling "lights out, Zepps about".

A visit to Saxmundham in the 1840s

Sylvia Lyon's (nee Lines) maternal grandfather wrote this account of his own father's visit to Saxmundham.

"My Father has told me, when his father used to drive into the town from Wenhaston Old Hall Farm to the market in Saxmundham, every time he had to pay one shilling (5p) at the Tollgate House. He would put his horse up at the Bell yard, and of course there was no Albion Street then, just meadows. Opposite was Mr Howlett's painting and plumber's workshop and that was all until you came to the mill.

Over to the right was an old farmhouse called Wingfield Chantry. It had a very handsome key with lovely work on it to lock the front door.

Saxmundham was practically self supporting. They made their own flour, brewed their own beer, made their own candles and leather for boots, and their own furniture and clocks. A very good clockmaker was called J. D. Bright."

Alice and the Lusitania

Alice Maud Lines (aunt of Sylvia Lyon) was born on 18th December 1896 in Saxmundham. In 1901, Alice lived with her family at Fairfield Road and by 1911, she was a kitchen maid in domestic service at Friston near Saxmundham.

After leaving school Alice went to London to train as a children's nurse and in January 1914 she responded to an advertisement.

WANTED
Young children's nurse willing to travel.

Adding two years to her age she was taken on by an American couple, Major and Mrs Pearl, and travelled with them to the USA.

In 1915 Major Pearl was summoned back to London to work at the US embassy.

The family, along with Alice, boarded the RMS Lusitania for its ill-fated return trip to Britain in May 1915.

Alice was in charge of Stuart, aged five, and Audrey, aged three months, whilst an under nurse looked after the two other children, Amy and Susan.

The German Embassy in New York had taken out newspaper advertisements warning people to not sail on any British or allied ships.

As the Lusitania rounded the southern coast of Ireland, it was struck by at least one German torpedo.

Alice testified to the British Inquiry that she had saved two of the Pearl children by bringing them with her to a lifeboat which was lowered in safety.

After three hours they were picked up by a trawler and taken to Queenstown.

The Lusitania sank in just 18 minutes with 1,200 casualties. The Germans claimed that sinking the ship was fair in war as they said it was transporting ammunition destined for the British war effort. It may also explain why the ship sunk so quickly if the ammunition exploded due to the torpedo strike.

After frantically searching for the rest of the family for several days, Alice was re-united with Major and Mrs Pearl, but sadly the other children and their nurse were never seen again.

Later, Alice's story changed ...

As she came on deck with her two charges, a sailor snatched Stuart and threw him into a lifeboat.

When she tried to follow, they held her back saying the boat was full. Clutching baby Audrey, She jumped into the sea and was ultimately rescued, fortunately, by the same lifeboat in which Stuart had been placed only minutes before.

Some of this story about Alice is based on research by Peter Engberg-Klarström.

Top: Alice Lines pictured in 1915

Above: Lusitania leaving New York on what would be her last voyage, 1915

Aline Aldous

Aline inherited Hurts Hall following the death of her brother, Squire Long. She was a forthright lady and took part in an oral history recording in the 1990s. The full recording can be heard by visiting the Museum.

Some of the things she talks about include the belief that her father was the first person in Suffolk to own a motor car and her mother couldn't hold outdoor summer parties because the smell from the river Fromus was so awful!

Before the days of town sewers there are records of outbreaks of disease.

It's interesting to note a tale from a resident of Benhall village who recalls that each year he would dig a new pit in the back garden and how the human fertiliser would work wonders on the home grown vegetables. Larger towns would have a Soil Man who would empty and take away the contents of back garden 'privies' each evening.

Ron Thompson

Ron moved to Saxmundham in 1929, when he was eight. The population was approximately 1,550. There were two doctor's surgeries, one stone mason, one funeral parlour, the gas works, sawmills, E.C. Bus Company, L.N.E.R., many unmade roads, no sewerage system and just six council houses. Ron's first job was at the Gas Works in Station Approach.

In 1939, at the age of 18, Ron was called up to join the army as Private Ron Thompson in the 4th Battalion, Suffolk Regiment (TA).

Ron was sent to east Asia in October 1941 but within 17 days he and his troop were taken as prisoners of war by the Japanese where he was forced to work on the infamous 'Bridge on the River Kwai'.

"We had more casualties than any other group because we were in a known Cholera belt and 30 men a day were dying"

Unlike many of his comrades he survived and after the war trained to be a plasterer. He went on to work for Reade of Aldeburgh as a builder and plasterer.

He was a keen football player and youth team coach and, like his father before him, he volunteered as a reserve fireman.

Chris Cousins

A familiar figure around the town in his role as dustman, Chris took the council cart to collect the rubbish with his horse 'Daisy'. Chris was recorded in the early 2000s, when he was 98yrs old, talking about his life and his small-holding in Street Farm Road. His recording can be heard at the Museum.

Top: Mrs Aline Aldous

Above: 18 year old Ron Thompson

Right: Chris Cousins pictured in 1968 at the top of Saxon Road with Daisy

HEALTHCARE

Ryder Richardsons

Left: Dr John Charles Ryder Richardson pictured in the early 20th century

Below: Prince Philip (left) with friends John and David Ryder Richardson

The Ryder-Richardson family provided healthcare services over several generations for Saxmundham residents at the Beeches, North Entrance.

A friend and frequent visitor was a young Prince Philip of Greece, the future Duke of Edinburgh; the boys' nannies were friends.

Local reminiscences include the doctors being a little hard of hearing and as you sat in the waiting room you could hear all about the other patients' ailments!

Another patient, this time at the dentists surgery, wondered why injections at afternoon appointments were more painful than those in the morning. He later discovered that the same needle was used all day and became blunt!

Doctor Collins also had a practice at the 'Chantry' in South Entrance.

SCHOOLS

Private Schools

Owen Haxell's 'School for Young Gentlemen' was located at Brook Cottage, North Entrance in the early 1800s.

Owen Haxell was known by the pupils as 'Custards'. Artist Henry Bright and sculptor Thomas Thurlow were both pupils, as was Dr David Richardson, many years later.

Mr Sparrow's Academy was located in 10-12 Albion Street from 1855 to 1881.

William Harvey, born in 1869, went to the school when he was 9 years old. He joined about 20 boys who walked each day from the surrounding villages. Friend Ernest rode in on a donkey from Snape.

'Mr Sparrow never used a blackboard and we had to take our slates up to him for correction. One boy nicknamed Soot Bags, because he wore a rusty black velvet suit, was an orphan and Mr Sparrow's particular butt. Two or three times a week he would flog the boy unmercifully striking him on his back, thighs or calves.'

Above: School for Young Gentlemen

Above right: Bridge House

Bottom right: White House School

William Harvey's son recollects that in 1954 a scar was still evident in his father's hand, left by a nail in the slate frame with which he was thrashed.

In the 1880s **Bridge House** was at the back of the Church House, opposite St Johns Church drive.

Mrs Goldsmith's grandmother instructed young ladies in household management. (Mrs Goldsmith was Saxmundham's first hairdresser.)

White House School was located in North Entrance, next to the Coach and Horses, (the area replaced by the Post Office in the 1950s).

It was run by Mrs Richenda Walker from 1869 to 1892. This was a Dame School, consisting of 20 girls aged 5-15 and two boys.

South Holme School was in Fairfield Road from 1908 until 1922.

The school was previously located in South Entrance at The Firs (1896-1903), then over the road in The Red House (1904-1907).

It was run by Kate and Edith Wells, daughters of William Wells, the ironmonger.

Arthur Crisp (of the stationers) attended the school between 1912 and 1917 and received a good 'grounding' in education.

Parham House School was located in Fairfield Road from 1948 to 1973.

Head teacher Barbara Russell was known affectionately as 'Auntie Barbara'. She was described as an excellent teacher and a workaholic. In 25 years running the school she only had one holiday, and only one pupil was known to have failed the 11+. This was a boarding and day school with 18 boarders and 45 day pupils.

Fairfield Preparatory School was located in North Entrance

Miss Henderson and Miss Partridge, known as 'Hen & Part', started the school in 1948 with eight pupils. By the time they retired in 1972 there were 80 pupils.

During the headship of Mr & Mrs Durdy the numbers rose to 100 with the added nursery facility. They were followed by Mr Parsons and finally Mr & Mrs Neve. The school closed in 1996.

Top left: South Holme School

Top right: South Holme teachers and pupils, 1918

Centre left: Fairfield Preparatory School

Bottom left: Parham House School

State Schools

'On the hill near the church is a neat school erected in 1836 by Squire Long who pays for the education of 70 poor boys and girls'.

White's Suffolk, 1844

In 1746 William Corbold agreed to pay £5 a year for the education of four children from Saxmundham, at **Benhall School**.

The first teachers of Saxmundham's first **Free School** were Joseph Austin and Mary Aldred.

In the 1850s it became known as the **National School**. A first floor was added in 1877 as a reading room.

The **National Infant School** was built on Church street in 1873. The first Mistress in charge was Miss Charlotte Ellis. The architecture of the building, opposite a major supermarket, is unchanged.

Saxmundham Board School was built in 1895 on Fairfield Road.

Two hundred children, along with parents, teachers and others, attended the opening ceremony where the children were given a 'sumptuous tea at 5d a head and were entertained by Mr Strode, a conjurer from London'.

Top: National Infant School

Centre right: Saxmundham County Modern School; note the surrounding fields

Right: Primary School, previously known as the Board School

The first headmaster was Mr Fillimore. Children aged 5-14 years were educated here, and it became known as the **Council School**. In the 1930s the older boys and girls had to walk from Benhall School to Saxmundham to do woodwork and cookery, respectively, once a week. Pupils from Rendham and Yoxford, who lived more than three miles away, were issued with bicycles.

In 1958 it became the **Primary School** when the **County Modern School** was built for pupils aged 11 to 15. The Primary school moved premises in 1995 to Brook Farm with Mr Murphy continuing as head teacher.

The first headmaster of **Saxmundham County Modern** was Mr Westthorpe with 292 pupils. Children who had passed the 11+ went to Leiston Grammar School.

One of the memorable occasions was a visit to the school by Gladys Aylward speaking about her life and work as a missionary in China.

In 1973, along with all schools in the county, education embarked on a three tier system and the 11+ exam was scrapped. **Saxmundham Middle School** educated 393 children aged 9-13; headteacher was Mr Rasmussen and there were 15 teaching staff. In 2012 education reverted back to the two tier system and the Middle School closed, with the **Seckford Education Trust School** opening on the site, educating all children aged 11-16.

THE CINEMA

During WW1 a projector on a trailer showed films in the Market Hall. In 1919 the **Kinema** was opened in the Salvation Army Hall, which was located on the High Street, near the Museum. Mr Punchard was the first manager and Flossie Bowers played the piano for the silent films.

As a school boy, Noel Vincent moved from London to live in Saxmundham and among his memoirs he recalls visiting the Kinema.

> *'We watched cartoons of aeroplanes dropping bombs on Kaiser Bill, and laughed at Charlie Chaplin. We sat in the ninepennies because rough boys sat in the fivepennies and threw orange peel. The authority of the usherette with her torch extended from the expensive seats at the back, used by young men and their girls, down to the ninepennies', but stopped there. Then it was every boy for himself!"*

In 1929 the Hall was used again by The Salvation Army, and years later some old films were discovered under a ramp.

The **Playhouse Cinema** in Church Street was officially opened on 11th November 1934 by Lord Cranbrook. It was mostly on one raked floor with a small gallery and was owned and managed by Captain Atkinson. The first film to be shown was *Melody in Spring*, supported by *Death Takes a Holiday*. Along with Sunday evening concerts with performers such as Jackie Trent and Joe Brown, it continued to show films and Saturday matinees.

One feature much appreciated by courting couples were the double seats, fondly known as cuddle seats. The experience of cinema-goers in Sax included the vibrations of heavy traffic on the A12, which ran through the town, the whistles from the nearby railway station and the beating of rain on the tin roof!

The cinema paid well from the beginning and the war brought plenty of custom from the neighbouring camps and aerodromes.

In 1945 Captain Atkinson died and Joan and Henry Foster took over the management of the cinema until 1962 when it finally closed and the building became a workshop for car dealer Smith and Wesby.

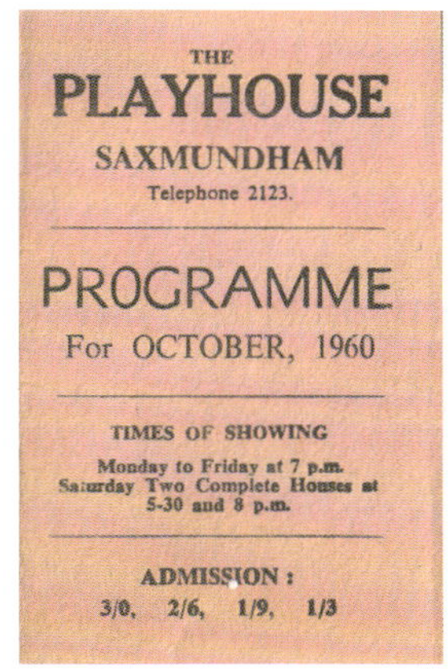

THE
PLAYHOUSE
SAXMUNDHAM
Telephone 2123.

PROGRAMME
For OCTOBER, 1960

TIMES OF SHOWING
Monday to Friday at 7 p.m.
Saturday Two Complete Houses at 5-30 and 8 p.m.

ADMISSION :
3/0, 2/6, 1/9, 1/3

1/- INCL. TAX Row L Seat No. 16
THE PLAYHOUSE
SAXMUNDHAM
RESERVED TICKET
MONDAY 27 DEC 1937

Top left: Aerial view of the site of the cinema

Top right: Playhouse Cinema

Above: 1960 Programme and 1937 ticket with its excise stamp

Left: Joan Foster in the box office

CELEBRATIONS

Right: Queen Victoria's Golden Jubilee Celebration Lunch, 1887

Near right: Bonfire being built for George V Silver Jubilee celebrations, 1935

Far right: George V Silver Jubilee Parade, 1935

Near right: Christmas party at the United Services Club, Albion Street, 1940s

Far right: Festival of Britain Fancy Dress Party, 1951

A memory from 1953, leading up to the Coronation, was the sight of three men, one dressed as a woman, playing a barrel organ. They went through every street in the town raising money for the Coronation fund to put on a children's tea party.

Near right: Morrie Bugg, George Cooper and Frank Boland, fund raising

Far right: 1962 Carnival

HISTORIC BUILDINGS

Carlton Hall

Carlton Hall was home to the Garret family, founders of the Leiston Longshop which manufactured agricultural equipment and steam powered vehicles. The family's tombs reside in the grounds of Carlton Church.

The hall was requisitioned for American servicemen during WWII but burnt down in the 1940s. The present 'Hall' is a modern reconstruction from around 2013 and provides several private apartments. The original servants' accommodation and the stable block remain.

The remains of the gamekeepers cottage, building debris and a partially filled-in well can be found in Carlton woods, in an area referred to as 'the peasantry' on old maps. This is often mistaken for the site of the old Bottle and Glass inn.

The Workhouse

A former Plomesgate workhouse was in Rendham Road close to Saxon Road. A 1777 report mentioned its capacity to house 60 occupants. By the 1880s it is referred to on maps as the "Old Workhouse".

Fairfield House

Along Harper's Lane, named after the former owner of Fairfield House, there is a tale of ghostly children seen playing in the grounds of Fairfield House. The house featured in the Bottle and Glass incident as the poor woman, Clara Barber, was taken there in a state of high distress after her son fell down a well.

Monks Cottages

Featured in the BBC programme *House Detectives*, Monks Cottages in South Entrance were originally one house. It's thought that the southern end was originally the kitchen area, which at some point caught fire and was rebuilt.

Top left: Carlton Hall

Above: Fairfield House

Left: Monks Cottages

Albion Mill

Above: Albion Mill in the various stages of its life

Local towns were self-sufficient in the growing of wheat and the milling of flour and many local towns and villages had their own mill.

Albion Mill was enlarged and raised higher as the town grew and blocked the wind draft to the mill.

A combination of the industrial revolution with more efficient milling and cheap imports of wheat from countries such as Russia led to the local mills falling into disuse.

The post mill was severely damaged in storms and was dismantled in 1907, later becoming a motor garage, before conversion to a private dwelling, and at one point it was offered as a holiday let.

Wingfield House

Wingfield House, a late 16th Century house with a 17th Century extension, was at one point separated into three cottages. It is situated behind the Market Place next to Old Bank House and has been recently restored.

Pest House

Situated on the southern edge of The Layers, the Pest House may date back to the Great Plague era and was a house of isolation intended to prevent the plague spreading. It is recorded in 1785 as the smallpox house. The census of 1841 shows Mr Deveraux Sawyer, 75, and his wife Elizabeth living at the Pest House.

Masonic Hall

A Masonic Order is recorded as meeting at the Bell Inn as early as 1816.

In 1934 the Earl of Stradbroke laid the foundation stone of the masonic hall in Chapel Road for Abif Lodge.

The Lodge bought an organ originally built and installed at Sibton Hall c1830. It was brought for the Saxmundham lodge in 1935 at a cost of £22.

The Aldeburgh Adair Lodge has shared the Saxmundham Masonic Hall building since the refurbishment of the Aldeburgh White Hart Hotel meant they had to move.

The Freemasons remain one of the UK's biggest charitable donors.

Left: Masonic Hall in Chapel Road

Below: A 1940s painting of Wingfield Chantry, by Harry Rowell

Park House

Eccentric twins Rhoisia and Bridget Copinger Hill lived in Park House, South Entrance. In 1931, as débutantes, they were presented at Court. Both were keen archaeologists and helped with the excavations at Sutton Hoo in the 1930s.

One of the twins secured temporary Christmas work at Harrods. Being identical they thought it would be 'fun' to work half a day each, and so one worked in the mornings and the other in the afternoons! When Harrods discovered this they were not well pleased that their security system had been breached!

The twins would throw interesting parties, and on one occasion a huge laundry basket was delivered in the middle of the party, full of fish and chips!

On snowy days Saxmundham folk will remember them skiing down the High Street to do their shopping.

Wingfield Chantry

Wingfield Chantry, also known as 'The Ancient House', was the seat of the Manor of Swans. An Elizabethan house, located behind what is now the Market Place car park, was demolished in 1949. A visitor in the 1940s remembers going with their mother to deliver a Chapel magazine and the door being opened by an old lady with her brother. It was said that it was unsafe to go upstairs, and that the house was haunted by a little man in waiter's dress!

CHURCHES AND CHAPELS

St John's Church

Above: 1848 etching alongside a photograph of the church today

Background: Stained glass window depicting the ascension of Jesus

St John's is the oldest recorded building in Saxmundham, mentioned in the Domesday survey of 1086. Sadly the last remains of the 11th century nave, including its Norman doorway and 15th century porch, disappeared in 1872 when the south aisle was extended.

The Swan Chapel in the South Chancel was founded in 1308 by Robert Swan who was Lord of the Manor. He was also the rector of Saxmundham from 1301 to the 1340s.

Saxmundham's 'wild-man of the woods', or Woodwose, can be found in images carved into the base of the font. In other churches these mysterious creatures can be seen as reliefs adorning the porch.

A Woodwose's club is said to represent unrepentant sinners, if held aloft, or sinners who have repented, if the club is lowered.

Above: Woodwose carving on the font

Right: Sundial carving in John Noller's tombstone

The 1873 pews were made from New Zealand kaurie pine. They replaced the old box pews, which were so tall that many folk could neither see or be seen! In 2017 the Victorian pews were replaced by chairs.

The large panels behind the altar, the reredos were carved in 1873 by Thomas Thurlow.

The six bells in the bell tower date back to 1480. In 1938 one of the bells was re-cast and all the bells re-hung, giving rise to this inscription, "Re-cast in 1938, Alfred Bowell made me and hung us all"!

The 19th Century stained glass windows throughout the church depict biblical events.

Inside and out there are memorials to local people, including the Long family.

In the churchyard is the large tomb of artist Thomas Thurlow and the interesting tombstone of John Noller. This has small inclined oblong recesses which form a sundial, the upper edge of which points exactly to the North Star. A morning dial is carved on the East face and an evening dial on the West face.

United Reformed Church

In the 1840s several members of the Rendham Chapel, who lived in Saxmundham, worked towards the building of a Congregational Chapel in Saxmundham. Businessmen William Wells and Isaac Ashford were foremost in leading the project.

It opened in 1850 at a cost of £1,400 and had seating for 400 people.

When the Congregational and English Presbyterian churches combined in 1972, the chapel became the United Reformed Church. The church is still in use, and the attached school room is well used by the community.

Salvation Army Hall

The Salvation Army Hall, 45 High Street, opened in 1892 seating 150 people. Between 1919 and 1929 the numbers were few and the hall was used as the 'Kinema'.

> *"During this time The Salvation Army was maintained by the town cobbler who lived in Mill Hole. He worked in an old railway carriage and on Saturday nights, resplendent in his Salvation Army uniform, he walked down to the Market Place and gave his address to anyone, or no-one. Come rain, fog or snow, Mr Jackson kept the faith. Occasionally he was joined by visiting Salvationists with voices and tambourines, but he never seemed to mind being a one-man way to salvation."*
>
> *Noel Vincent*

The hall re-opened again for use by the Salvation Army. During WW2 it was used as a WRVS canteen for servicemen, and reopened in 1946, finally closing in the 1990s due to structural faults. It has since been redeveloped for private housing.

Baptist Chapel

In Albion Street, the building now housing the Ex-Servicemen's and Social Club was once the Chapel for 'Particular Baptists'.

The chapel was built in 1854 costing £400 and seating 200 hundred people. The Baptistery is thought to be still under the floor to this day.

The Chapel closed in the mid 1930s. It was bought first by Rand Fisher and then by trustees of the British Legion for use as a social club.

Above: United Reformed Church

Left: Sax Social Club, previously the Baptist Chapel

SHOPS

A few examples of the many different types of shop in Saxmundham, which along with the businesses in town, made it largely self sufficient.

The earliest local minted currency, produced in the 17th Century, were the Trade Tokens. Saxmundham produced trade tokens for John Hunt, Apothecary, in 1669, Nicholas Shepherd, Draper and Woollens, in 1673 and for Thomas Knight.

High Street

Above: An example of a Saxmundham Trade Token

Near right: No. 39, showing Flatman's Ironmongers, 1857-1946

"An early 19th Century yellow brick house, the rear was originally part of Number 7, Market Place."

Far right: No. 33-35, A.E. Ellis, Boot Warehouse, 1906

Near right: No. 30, 1891 George Easey, Saddler and Harness Maker, followed by his son Horace who died in 1969. The business was taken over by C. Smith, known as 'Emperor' Smith. After his death in 1978 his widow ran the shop. Previously, in 1864 Christopher Newton, Chemist.

Far right: No. 14, International Stores

Near right: No. 7, Gobbit's Furnishing shop, renovated by the Co-Op in 1933. On re-opening day each customer was presented with a free chicken!

Far right: No. 16, A.M. Crisp, Baker and Refreshments

Above: No. 25-27, Crisp's Booksellers, Printers, Stationers (1868-2007); previously Brightly family (1830-67)

Far left: No. 11, Hartley's Grocery, (1950s-70), previously from 1850-60, Grocer and Silk Merchant followed by Surgeon, Doctor and Grocers

Near left: No. 46, in 1830 John Ridley's Ironmongers, joined by William Wells then taken over by Richard Wells

Left: No. 4, Hayward family, Plumber and Builders' Merchants 1860 -1990; previously, Whaley & Beard, Plumber and Builders' Merchants (1830s)

No. 2, Scarff's Greengrocer (1916-70), previously Christian Knowledge Depot (1875-88), Walter Lee, Tobacconist (1900-15)

Right: No. 8, Job Dalby, Butcher, 1879-1908; a butcher's business remains on this site

"I remember farmer Mr Sampson from Benhall delivering milk in a churn. Hanging from the churn were ladles of different measures and my mother would bring out a jug to be filled."

Richard Wills Crisp

South Entrance

Right: The Wine Merchants, c1910, under H. Waller's management, later Hunter & Oliver in 1940s-60s, then for a time a Threshers off-licence.

Albion Street

Right: Mrs Harriet Packard's Grocery, 1914-65

"Mr Akers who owned a general store in Albion Street, was known to ride his bike around Saxmundham on Sunday afternoons and sell ice-creams from a cold box on the front of his bike; pre-dating ice-cream vans in Saxmundham!"

Richard Wills Crisp

Market Place

Above left: No 6 & 8, Brighton and Hartley, grocers, outfitters & drapers

Above right: No. 22, C.E. Clarke Saddlery, 1890s

Left: No. 9, Alfie Proudfoot, AKA The Stilts-man

"Each evening at dusk the lamplighter would light the individual gas lamps in the High Street and Market Place and return around midnight to turn them off."

Richard Wills Crisp

Far left: No. 16, Hubbard Electrical store, previously the Star pub which lost its licence in the 1920s as it was felt there were too many pubs in town leading working men astray!

Near left: No. 22, Arthur Davey's fuel office; Mrs Miller also sold art supplies here, whilst taking orders for coal

A snapshot of 1784

"I remember that bananas were transported from Jamaica and the Canary Isles and brought to Saxmundham, where wholesaler Mr. Stebbings would ripen them. This was an intricate procedure. Next to his home in South Entrance were six rooms of differing temperatures for the ripening of the bananas. The rooms were heated by gas jets."

Richard Wills Crisp

Historic shops and business show how East Anglian towns such as Saxmundham were largely self sufficient.

The town's livestock market supplied four slaughter houses which in turn supplied local butchers and a tannery at South Entrance which is said to have been the source of very bad odours.

In 1784, for example, the tannery supplied leather to local businesses such as shoe maker J. Cable and saddle maker William George. Clothes shops included Thomas Gurden, J. Clarke and Isaac Matthew. Hats were available from James Brewer.

Shops and businesses listed in Saxmundham in 1784:

Isaac Ablet, *Carpenter & Builder*
James Brewer, *Hatter*
J. Cable, *Shoe-maker*
J. Clarke, *Glover & Breeches-maker*
William Cooper, *Surgeon & Apothecary*
Thomas Farrer, *Brazier & Watch-maker*
William George, *Saddler*
Thomas Gurden, *Draper & Haberdasher*
John Knights, *Bookseller & Distributor of Stamps*
Isaac Mayhew, *Glover & Breeches-maker*
Robert Meller, Brazier, *Plumber & Glazier*
Meteor & Michell, *Attorneys at Law*
Thomas Sackett, *Innkeeper at the Bell*
William Schuldham, *Attorney at Law*
Miss Smith, *Milliner & Agent to Royal Exchange Insurance Office*
Samuel Sustiner, *White Hart Inn*
Miss Swaler, *Draper & Milliner*
Thomas Symonds, *Surgeon*
William Wood, *Attorney at Law*

WAR YEARS

During the first world war, The Layers in Saxmundham was a regular camping ground for the 6th Cyclist Battalion whilst Carlton Park hosted a recruitment desk, camping huts, cook house and other ancillary buildings for troops.

Far left: British Red Cross detachment, 1914

Left: Troops outside Market Hall, Arthur Henry Crisp on the drum, 1914

Far left: Military Sports at Carlton Park, 1915

Left: 6th (Cyclist) Battalion, part of the Suffolk Regiment 1915

Far left: Haywards' builders erecting temporary accommodation for the troops

Left: Troops outside one of the huts

Far left: Pontoons in South Entrance, 1915

Left: Members of the Fire Brigade outside their new station in Rendham Road, 1915

Far left: 'Gas Pipe Cavalry' kitchen 1916

Left: An army barber shop

Right: Armoured Train C in service near Saxmundham in August 1940

During World War Two, Carlton Hall was requisitioned for the Americans. Carlton Park had an encampment of huts and the main guard house is still in place, viewable from the road.

Right: Saxmundham's Observer Corps, c1940

Hurts Hall was requisitioned for the soldiers of the nearby great guns at Sternfield but was also home to Major-General Sir Percy Hobart. Having been marginalised and viewed as a bit of a maverick, he was reinstated by Churchill and tasked to provide some uniquely modified equipment to assist in the D-Day landings. Called 'Hobarts Funnies', some worked and some didn't!

Right: Parade passing the Market Hall, c1943

The great guns at Sternfield had a range of fire from Walberswick down the coast to Slaughden.

Five bombs fell on Saxmundham during one night of the war. At the time the town had the gas works and BP fuel depot close to the station. Fortunately, the bombs didn't go off, or the town probably wouldn't have retained Market Place!

The Parish Room, a former building off station approach, decorated for Christmas, 1914

FINALLY, SENT TO ROOM 101

Top right: Helen Richardson, sister of Dr John, took this photo of a German with his dancing bear in Fairfield Road in the early 1900s; his livelihood was touring local towns and villages and they disappeared in 1914

Centre right: Saxmundham Minstrel Troupe, 1910

Below: Col. Alfred Bloomfield of Great Glemham as a District Commissioner in India killed the only recorded flesh-eating elephant; on his death the trophies of trunk and skull were auctioned by Messrs Ashfords

Background: Members of the hunt gather in Market Place

Being drummed out of the village

The late Jane Hawksley of Sternfield remembered this incident from her childhood in the early 1920s.

"A pregnant, unmarried girl from the village was forced to walk through the village street whilst the local inhabitants banged saucepans and frying pans to mark her 'disgrace'.

I particularly remember an old crone with her face twisted with fury and disgust.

The girl then had to leave the village and went to stay with people in Wickham Market."

Another unmarried lady in Kelsale, who fell pregnant, committed suicide. She lies buried in the furthest corner of the church grounds in an unmarked grave.

Every town has moments in its history that it perhaps wouldn't like to think about and Saxmundham is no exception. Images record activities now deemed unacceptable or even illegal.

Saxmundham residents were entertained by a bear forced to dance and act unnaturally, and it wasn't unusual for a group of performers to wear 'black face' before they danced and sang, something now frowned upon.

Obviously we cannot, and perhaps should not, delete our past but who knows which artistic performance, activity or sport we currently enjoy might be sent to Room 101 in a hundred years time?